The Way of Pilgrimage is like a new best friend! You can walk right into its welcoming presence and begin at once to find fresh truths sprouting up from ancient sources. It will become a trusted guide for those who accompany youth and young adults on their paths of meaning-making.

It promises especially satisfying moments for leaders who wish to engage others in the rhythmic paces of spiritual formation. The weekly gatherings show us how to move from deeply ingrained habits of content-based Bible study into soul-tending practices of contemplation and community that open us to transformation.

—THE REVEREND DR. DORI BAKER
Author, *Doing Girlfriend Theology: God-Talk with Young Women*
United Methodist pastor and professor of youth ministry and Christian education

As an organization completely dedicated to the art of pilgrimage, we are overjoyed with *The Way of Pilgrimage* resources. *The Way of Pilgrimage* is a comprehensive and passionate guide that brings us back to our ancient heritage of pilgrimage through modern eyes and practical application.

Utilize these resources to teach your youth God's unique design of our lives as journeys of exploration and adventure. There is no better resource available to date that prepares your teens as lifelong pilgrims.

—SHAWN SMALL
Executive director, Wonder Voyage Pilgrimages

Finally—a spiritual resource for youth and young adults with depth and meaning! Upper Room Books continues its Companions in Christ series with an insightful and creative journey for Generation Next. I love this resource!

—BO PROSSER
Coordinator for congregational life, Cooperative Baptist Fellowship

This inspiring resource meets participants wherever they are in their spiritual walks and gently moves them toward a deeper understanding of their own pilgrimage. In the context of a Christian community of travelers, participants shed light on the most unexamined corners of their souls. . . .

As an educator of secondary students, I greatly appreciate how consistently this text works to provide spiritual development activities for every kind of learner—from still meditation to verbal expression to artistic interpretations.

—JESSICA ROSENTHAL
United Methodist educator and youth helper

The Way of Pilgrimage is a wonderful doorway into the spiritual life. Like the bountiful feast that God sets before us, these volumes are full of wisdom and blessing. Those who accept the challenge to walk with Christ will benefit greatly from this guide. Its exercises are both simple and rich. At every point, the members of the group are encouraged to journey into the heart of God.

—THE REVEREND DANIEL WOLPERT
Pastor, First Presbyterian Church, Crookston, Minnesota
Codirector, Minnesota Institute of Contemplation and Healing (MICAH)
Author, *Leading a Life with God*

A COMPANIONS *in Christ* Resource

COMPANIONS ON THE PILGRIMAGE

PARTICIPANT'S BOOK

Steve Matthews

 VOLUME **4**

UPPER ROOM BOOKS®
NASHVILLE

COMPANIONS ON THE PILGRIMAGE
Participant's Book Volume 4
Copyright © 2007 by Upper Room Books®
All rights reserved.
The Upper Room® Web site: http://www.upperroom.org

Cover design: Left Coast Design, Portland, OR
Interior design: Gore Studio, Inc., Nashville, TN
Typesetting: PerfecType, Nashville, TN
First printing: 2007

ISBN-13   978-0-8358-9837-9
ISBN-10   0-8358-9837-7

At the time of publication all Web sites referenced in this book were valid. However, due to the fluid nature of the Internet some addresses may have changed or the content may no longer be relevant.

LIBRARY OF CONGRESS CATALOGING-IN-PUBLICATION DATA
Matthews, Steve.
  Companions on the pilgrimage : participant's book / Steve Matthews.
      p. cm.—(The way of pilgrimage ; v. 4)
  Includes bibliographical references.
  1. Christian youth—Religious life. 2. Fellowship—Religious aspects—Christianity. 3. Spiritual formation. I. Matthews, Steve. Way of pilgrimage. II. Title.
  BV4531.3.M419 2007
  263'.041—dc22   2007003691

Printed in the United States of America

CONTENTS

MEET THE WRITER

Steve Matthews has served as a youth minister for thirteen years. Currently he works at St. Paul's Episcopal Church in Richmond, Virginia (one of the partner churches in the Youth Ministry and Spirituality Project). In his role at St. Paul's he has led four youth pilgrimages—three to Ireland and one to Italy. He has an MDiv from Baptist Theological Seminary at Richmond and an MA in clinical psychology from Western Carolina University. Steve also has a diploma in spiritual direction from the San Francisco Theological Seminary. He loves to travel and enjoys quiet walks in the woods.

ACKNOWLEDGMENTS

The Way of Pilgrimage is a new adventure in spiritual formation for a new generation of Companions in Christ groups. The original twenty-eight-week *Companions in Christ* resource was published by Upper Room Books in spring 2001. The ensuing Companions in Christ series has been designed to create settings in which people can respond to God's call to an ever-deepening communion and wholeness in Christ—as individuals, as members of a small group, and as part of a congregation. Building upon the *Companions in Christ* foundational vision, *The Way of Pilgrimage* is written for a younger audience of senior-high youth and first-year college students.

The first consultation for developing *The Way of Pilgrimage* took place in Nashville in February 2005. We are deeply grateful to these consultants and to the writers of the Leader's Guide and Participant's Books: Sally Chambers, Kyle Dugan, Steve Matthews, Craig Mitchell, Jeremy Myers, Jonathon Norman, Kara Lassen Oliver, Gavin Richardson, Ciona Rouse, Jessica Rosenthal, Daniel Wolpert, and Jenny Youngman. Special thanks to Stephen Bryant, visionary leader of the Companions in Christ resources and publisher of Upper Room Ministries. He developed and wrote all the daily exercises found in this book.

We are also indebted to those who reviewed the early manuscript and offered their insights on theology and pilgrimage: The Reverend Matthew Corkern, Christ Church Cathedral Episcopal Church in Nashville, Tennessee; Sally Chambers, St. Paul's Episcopal Church in Franklin, Tennessee; and Jeremy Myers, Augsburg College in Minneapolis, Minnesota.

The following churches and groups tested portions of early versions of *The Way of Pilgrimage*:

- Belmont United Methodist Church in Nashville, Tennessee (leader: Jessica Rosenthal)
- Wesley United Methodist Church in Coral Gables, Florida (leader: the Reverend César J. Villafaña)

- First United Methodist Church in Hendersonville, Tennessee (leader: Gavin Richardson)
- North Park University in Chicago, Illinois (leaders: Susan Braun and Jodi DeYoung)
- Milford United Methodist Church in Milford, Michigan (leader: Sherry Foster)
- Westminster Presbyterian Church in Eugene, Oregon (leaders: Jen Butler and Katie Stocks)
- St. Paul's Episcopal Church in Richmond, Virginia (leader: Steve Matthews)
- SoulFeast 2006 Youth Program in Lake Junaluska, North Carolina (leader: Ciona Rouse)

The Companions in Christ Staff Team
Upper Room Ministries

INTRODUCTION

You have made us for yourself, O Lord,
and our heart is restless till it rests in you.

—Saint Augustine

We are a pilgrim people, always moving, always wanting more, never satisfied, never full, and never finished. We are a pilgrim people.

Throughout the scriptures, God continually reminds us of our pilgrim hearts and calls us back to the path that leads us home. The psalmist declares, "For I am . . . a traveler passing through, as my ancestors were before me" (Ps. 39:12, NLT). And the letter to the Hebrews says it quite simply: We are "strangers and pilgrims on the earth" (11:13, NKJV). The word *pilgrim* comes from the Latin word meaning "resident alien." This world is not our home. Our life here on earth is just one stop on this all-encompassing pilgrimage, a physical and spiritual journey home to the One to whom we truly belong. We *are* a pilgrim people.

A "great cloud" of pilgrims travels with us. Some are pilgrims who have gone before us whom we no longer see, and many travel beside us in this world. All can become our companions on the road. We are a part of a great lineage of pilgrims witnessing to the path that leads to God and life. One thing we learn on this journey is that we are part of a much bigger story. It is a story that precedes us and that continues after us.

Traveling companions are essential to pilgrimage: those we set off with; those we meet along the way; and those who return home with us. These companions are gifts from God for our journey. They are guides and encouragers, cheerleaders who root for us. They pat our back and hold our hand. These traveling friends enhance the journey and point to the footsteps of all those pilgrims who have traveled this road before us. Through these companions, God tells us that we don't walk this road alone.

God calls each of us to our own pilgrimage and then gives us the companionship of other pilgrims who are also on their own journey. So side by side we travel, looking not toward each other but forward to the journey ahead and the God we each seek. Before we begin, here are a few reminders for the road:

There is a difference between being a tourist and being a pilgrim.
Just as we can travel to holy places as a tourist, not fully engaged or fully present, we also can walk this spiritual pilgrimage of faith as a tourist. Tourists may take snapshots of places along the way and yet still keep their hearts far removed, offering empty words to those they meet. Tourists also may be here only for the community and not the journey. *This is a journey for pilgrims.*

Companions along the way are essential to pilgrimage.
Keep in mind that even though we travel with others, each pilgrim must make his or her own journey. As fellow pilgrims we journey side by side, looking out together for the One we seek.

Each weekly gathering is a stop along the way.
Each gathering is space carved out and made holy. When we gather together, the gateway between God and us seems wider, and the intersection of heaven and earth more apparent. Each gathering is a place that says, *Welcome, pilgrims. Welcome to this respite. Welcome to this holy place.*

Rhythm is part of our daily routine as pilgrims.
In medieval times, pilgrims would set out on their journey in exactly the same way. Ritual and repetition were intrinsic to pilgrimage. And because pilgrims followed the same path, we can follow medieval pilgrim trails today in Europe and in the Holy Land. Every Good Friday pilgrims walk the way of the cross, the same path Jesus walked to his death (according to tradition). The repetition and rhythm of the daily exercises and readings are essential to this participant's book. So stick with them, and you will find that particular prayers, scriptures, and practices that are repeated through our journey will begin to sink from your head down to your heart; they will become as familiar and comforting as wearing a favorite old pair of shoes.

Pilgrimage is about being present in the present.

This pilgrimage is about waking up and paying attention to our lives. It also involves remembering our past. As we live our days awake to God in prayer, we will become present to God and to life.

This is a journey of the heart as well as the head.

In this journey, prayer, conversation, listening, reading, noticing, and looking are transformed from activities of the mind to practices of the heart.

You are invited to engage in the exercises each day and read the daily readings. The shaded paragraphs you'll find in the readings offer an essential idea in the passage. Be sure to get yourself a journal to use for exercises, reflections, and group meetings.

So welcome, pilgrim! May you journey faithfully and with integrity. May you make great strides, though this pilgrimage does not literally go far. As you learn to listen for the word of God, allowing it to guide you on this way, may you come to know who you really are and what you truly seek. And may Christ "dwell in your hearts through faith, as you are being rooted and grounded in love. . . . May [you] have the power to comprehend, with all the saints, what is the breadth and length and height and depth, and to know the love of Christ that surpasses knowledge, so that you may be filled with all the fullness of God" (Eph. 3:17-19).

Welcome home. Welcome to *The Way of Pilgrimage*.

—Sally Chambers
Coauthor, *The Way of Pilgrimage* Leader's Guide

This week you will have time to revisit some of the giants of our faith story. If you flipped through the Bible like a family photo album, you would see Noah, Moses, and Jesus. In this resource, you will also meet lesser-known members of our family, such as Saint Francis and Clare. As you read and pray this week, get to know these ancestors of our faith, learn from them, and imagine them walking with you on this pilgrimage.

AN ENCOUNTER WITH FRANCIS BERNARDONE

Day 1 Exercise

READ HEBREWS 11:1-12, 32-40.

> *By faith Noah, warned by God about events as yet unseen, respected the warning and built an ark to save his household; by this he condemned the world and became an heir to the righteousness that is in accordance with faith. By faith Abraham obeyed when he was called to set out for a place that he was to receive as an inheritance; and he set out, not knowing where he was going.—Hebrews 11:7-8*

REFLECT Hebrews 11 is a litany of men and women who "through faith conquered kingdoms, administered justice, obtained promises, shut the mouths of lions, quenched raging fire, escaped the edge of the sword, won strength out of weakness, became mighty in war, and put foreign armies to flight" (11:33-34).

Name some men and women who have become your heroes of the faith. Is it their everyday lives or an extraordinary act of faith that inspires you? How have they assisted you in understanding and living your faith?

PRAY Give thanks to God for the saints in your life.

ACT Think of a living person you recognize as a "saint" but who may not receive attention or appreciation for his or her faithfulness. Do something today to thank this person.

Day 1   Reading

Every time we inhale, we commune with all the saints who have come before us and walk beside us. Some of these saints are common, everyday people whose stories we may never know. They are people who touch lives with their faithfulness and kindness in seemingly anonymous ways—people in church pews, neighbors, perhaps great-great-grandparents we never knew. These are "ordinary" saints who change the world day by day with their love for others.

Francis of Assisi was one such saint. In the early thirteenth century, Francis Bernardone lived a life of prosperity and wealth in the medieval hill town of Assisi, Italy. Young Francis yearned for the romance, prestige, and power of knighthood. By the time he turned twenty, he had already fought in battles with neighboring city-states. War eventually ended in capture, illness, and disillusionment for him. But Francis pressed on toward the chivalrous allure of knighthood.

As time passed, Francis grew tired and weary. The familiar questions, *What am I to do with my life?* and *What is my purpose?* must have crept into his consciousness as knighthood lost its romance. In his nighttime dreams and daytime wonderings he began to sense that God was speaking to him. Francis felt called by God to leave the battlefield and to return to Assisi.

His pilgrimage toward God took a new turn. Upon returning to Assisi, Francis spent nearly a year praying about what it would mean for him to follow God's will. Praying in the ruined chapel of San Damiano with an icon of Jesus on the cross, Francis heard God asking him to repair God's house, which was in ruin. Francis had found his calling.

BELOVED COMMUNITY TOGETHER IN ASSISI

Day 2 Exercise

READ MATTHEW 17:1-8.

> *Six days later, Jesus took with him Peter and James and his brother John and led them up a high mountain, by themselves. And he was transfigured before them, and his face shone like the sun, and his clothes became dazzling white.—Matthew 17:1-2*

REFLECT Notice how in prayer Jesus enjoyed spiritual fellowship with saints of old in conversation that transcended time and space. Enveloped by the bright cloud of God's eternal presence, two disciples with Jesus experienced the same fellowship, and so can we.

Name one or two spiritual giants of old (from the Bible or from Christian history) whom you feel particularly drawn to or would like to connect with. Then list one or more subjects you would like to talk about with them.

PRAY Imagine Jesus leading you up the mountain into God's presence with him. Imagine Jesus standing in communion and conversation with some of the greatest and most faithful human beings of all time. Which persons do you become aware of? What conversation do you overhear? What is Jesus saying to you or showing you through this experience?

ACT Google one or two spiritual giants that came to mind and learn something new about each one.

Day 2 Reading

The high school juniors and seniors from my church had been studying the lives of Francis and Clare (more on Clare to come) for a year, so it was with great excitement that twelve of us (nine youth and three adults) boarded a plane for Italy in July 2002. There are lots of different ways to travel to Italy. We could have traveled alone for the sense of adventure. We could have traveled with family and friends. We might also have chosen to join a tour group from school. But we chose to approach our ten days in Italy as a community of Christian pilgrims.

We arrived in Assisi, Italy, on a hot summer day and settled into our accommodations in the Monastero Santa Colette hospitality house. Our rooms were within the old city walls, and from our balconies we looked out onto the beautiful countryside and Umbrian plain below.

That first night in Assisi we walked up the steps to the old city center and treated ourselves to gelato (ice cream). In the piazza, we observed young people playing guitars on the church steps, busy street-side cafés, friends and couples walking arm in arm—it was romantic and invigorating. After over a year of fund-raising and preparation, we were finally in Italy! We walked the piazza and looked at the church dedicated to Mary, which had in pre-Christian times been a Roman temple for the goddess Minerva. It occurred to us that these were the same streets Francis walked over seven hundred years ago, that he too had climbed these church steps. We were amazed by the layers of history everywhere in Assisi.

We anticipated ten transforming days and welcomed Assisi as our home away from home. We would explore the important sites of the city and listen for what the saints of old had to teach us. Sometimes we would linger in places that seemed holy. We would worship together and laugh together. We would also find moments of solitude. With all of our senses, we yearned to be transformed by this ancient town and those who had inhabited its walls.

PILGRIMS LED BY LOVE

Day 3 Exercise

READ EXODUS 13:17-22.

The LORD went in front of them in a pillar of cloud by day, to lead them along the way, and in a pillar of fire by night, to give them light, so that they might travel by day and by night.—Exodus 13:21

REFLECT This passage describes how the Lord led our ancestors in the faith—the Israelites—out of Egypt and through the wilderness. Think about cloud and fire as metaphors for the way God loves and leads you through your wilderness periods; then ponder the people who make God's love and guidance visible to you.

Draw a picture of a big cloud over the hot wilderness days of your life. Think of how clouds protect you from the sun, provide rain and relief. When have you felt without direction or burnt by circumstances in your life? Where have you found relief when you thought you couldn't make it? Who has served as the protective cloud in your life? Write their names in your cloud picture. Now draw an image of fire. Ponder how fire gives light in darkness and warmth in cold. Who has served as a light of guidance or a fire to rekindle your courage and hope? Write their names in your flame image.

PRAY Which image of God's presence works best for you in prayer—cloud or fire? Close your eyes and picture a spiritual cloud over your life by day, covering you with love and guiding you in the way that leads to life. Then picture a flame of fire in your nighttimes, when the way is darkest. Look and listen for God's guidance.

ACT When you see clouds in the sky today, remember the presence of God with our ancient ancestors through time and God's presence with you now.

Day 3 Reading

Pilgrimages take all kinds of shapes and forms. People may travel to ancient holy sites like Rome, Jerusalem, and Mecca. People may return to family graveyards for reunions and picnics. High school and college reunions can be a form of pilgrimage as we journey back in time to places and people that have been important to us.

Pilgrimage involves movement. In the movie *Phenomenon*, the character George Malley (played by John Travolta) experiences a major transformation that challenges all his relationships and what he knows about himself. George's life is moving faster than ever, and he is confused. At one point, George looks up at the trees swaying in the wind, and out of the stillness he says reflectively, "Everything is on its way to somewhere." Whether we like it or not, life continually moves in us and around us, and we are called to make choices about our path through life. Even not choosing sets us on a course.

To be on pilgrimage means that we choose to move in a certain direction. We choose a quest, a destination, a way of being—we make a choice.

For Christians the choice is first and foremost to open our hearts to God's love shown in Jesus and to trust the belovedness that was ours from the beginning. This love at the core of our being draws us on pilgrimage. Like the children of Israel who saw God's faithfulness in the wilderness clouds, we look to the "cloud of witnesses" (Heb. 12:1) past and present to remind us that God faithfully accompanies us. From these saints, ordinary and extraordinary, we gather inspiration and strength for the journey.

For George Malley transformation was difficult. He didn't understand the changes he was experiencing, and many of his friends abandoned him because they couldn't understand what he was going through either. Our transformation in Christ is no easier. But when Christian community is at its best, we are accompanied and encouraged in our growth by the saints of old and by one another. We are all on this pilgrimage together.

THE INVISIBLE GOD BECOMES VISIBLE

Day 4 Exercise

READ JOHN 3:1-10.

Jesus answered, "Very truly, I tell you, no one can enter the kingdom of God without being born of water and Spirit. What is born of the flesh is flesh, and what is born of the Spirit is spirit."—John 3:5-6

REFLECT Notice how Jesus speaks of the movement of the Spirit of God in our lives as wind that blows where it chooses; we can hear, feel, and even see its effects, but its origins remain mysterious. Where do you hear, feel, or see the wind of God in your life? Is it a gentle breeze or a storm?

Picture the things that make wind visible: clouds moving across the sky, trees moving, leaves blowing about, and so forth. Who are the people that sometimes make the wind of God's Spirit visible for you and reveal the direction it is blowing?

PRAY Stand and reach your arms and hands out wide like a sail. Open your body and soul to God like the sail of a boat before a steady and promising wind. Feel the wind of the Spirit; sense where love will lead you as long as you hoist your sail.

ACT When you feel the wind today, ask God where the Spirit is blowing you.

Day 4 Reading

As a child I was intrigued by clouds. In the summer, my sister and I would lie in the grass and watch the fluffy pillars morph into dragons and cats, sunflowers and eagles. Sometimes I would watch dark clouds form on the horizon. In the summer these clouds might mean an outdoor adventure was about to be rained out. The clouds might signal us to get out of the pool because a storm was brewing. But in the winter these moisture-laden blankets were a blessing, because they often brought snow and unexpected vacations from school. I even loved fog. When driving through the foggy mountains, I was giddy (unlike my more responsible parents)—we were driving through the clouds. What could be better?

Meteorologically speaking, clouds are just hydrogen and oxygen, just air on its way to becoming water. Clouds form when the air rises and cools to form tiny droplets. When a bunch of tiny droplets group together, we get clouds. I guess you could say that clouds are a visual reminder that we are swimming around in air—life-giving air. Clouds make the unseen visible. In clouds, invisible air takes form as water vapor.

In scriptures we see God's spirit referred to as air. God's spirit is likened to wind (*ruach* in Hebrew) and breath (*pneuma* in Greek)—wind and breath, two forms of invisible air. If God is like air, then God's spirit must be everywhere. Wherever our pilgrim path takes us, God is already there. But, like air, God is invisible. With each breath we are invited to trust that God is walking with us. God is always behind, beside, and before—always a companion drawing us to God's very heart.

While we cannot see wind or breath directly, we can see their effects in the world and in our own bodies. So it is with God's spirit. We can learn to recognize the effects of the Holy Spirit in our hearts and our communities. And while God may be an invisible presence moving mysteriously in our lives, the "cloud of witnesses" makes God visible and tangible in our journeys of faith.

GOD IS PRESENT THROUGH OTHERS

Day 5 Exercise

READ HEBREWS 12:1-2.

*Therefore, since we are surrounded by so great a cloud of witnesses . . .
let us run with perseverance the race that is set before us, looking to
Jesus the pioneer and perfecter of our faith.—Hebrews 12:1-2*

REFLECT As the scripture says, "we are surrounded by so great a cloud
of witnesses." Draw two clouds over the landscape of your life: a dark cloud
and a bright cloud. In the dark cloud, list people or influences that darken
your way, discourage you, and do not help you trust God's faithfulness.

In the bright cloud, "a cloud of witnesses," list people and influences
that brighten your way, encourage you to reach for the promise in your life,
and help you trust God's faithfulness. What are the most important lessons
you learn from living under each cloud?

PRAY Enter into God's presence as though you were entering a cloud of
love filled with those people who make up your personal cloud of witnesses.
Pray for each person and feel that person's prayers for you.

ACT If you feel like you are living under your "dark cloud" today, seek
out one person who you know will brighten your day.

Day 5 Reading

In the book of Exodus God is present to a pilgrim people in the form of a cloud. These people are leaving slavery in Egypt to inhabit a new and Promised Land—a fertile land that offers peace and freedom just beyond the Jordan River. The cloud guides and protects them: "The Lord went in front of them in a pillar of cloud by day, to lead them along the way, and in a pillar of fire by night, to give them light, so that they might travel by day and by night" (Exod. 13:21).

What an amazing way to reassure a people on pilgrimage through a desert. It's as if God said, "Look up; follow the cloud. Remember, I am with you." With each passing day the people must have grown more confident in God's provision and the vision of the unseen Promised Land to which they were headed. Do we dare trust that the pilgrim's way with all its joys, challenges, and missed turns will lead us to the abundant life of the Spirit? The stories of our pilgrim ancestors proclaim a resounding yes!

The author of the book of Hebrews points to the people who have witnessed God's faithfulness. It is quite the hall of fame (and faith): Noah, Abraham, Sarah, Isaac, Jacob, Joseph, Moses, Rahab, Gideon, and Samuel, among others. These names represent stories of trial, of challenge and mistakes, of faithlessness and faithfulness. They were not perfect people, but their stories illustrate that God does indeed accompany us as we step through time. The writer states, "Therefore, since we are surrounded by so great a cloud of witnesses, let us also lay aside every weight and the sin that clings so closely, and let us run with perseverance the race that is set before us, looking to Jesus the pioneer and perfecter of our faith, who for the sake of the joy that was set before him endured the cross" (Heb. 12:1-2). The saints of our faith witness to Jesus, who pioneers our way home to God. They encourage us to keep following his path into the heart of divine love.

Many people travel this road with us, but there are a select few without whom we could not complete the journey. This week you will have time to name those friends who love you unconditionally, who help you and protect you, and are willing to tell you the truth. These "soul friends" are particular gifts from God. Remember them by name this week as you read, pray, and journal.

DISCOVERING SPIRITUAL FRIENDS

Day 1   Exercise

READ 1 SAMUEL 18:1-4; 23:15-18.

When David had finished speaking to Saul, the soul of Jonathan was bound to the soul of David, and Jonathan loved him as his own soul.
—1 Samuel 18:1

REFLECT The stories of David and Jonathan illustrate the gift and joy of genuine friendship. Identify the qualities of both natural and spiritual friendship that you see here.

Think about what you look for in a friend. What characteristics are you drawn to? What do you believe draws your friends to you?

PRAY Spend time in prayer giving thanks to God for your true friends.

ACT Act like a real friend today to someone you know, expressing those character traits you seek in a good friend.

Day 1 Reading

A few people I know like to travel alone, but the vast majority prefer to travel in the company of friends. When traveling, especially on long trips, I generally choose my best friends to go along. For the sake of our conversation on pilgrimage, we might call these my "spiritual friends."

For Francis of Assisi, true spiritual friends came to him as his call emerged. Like fog slowly lifting from the valley below Assisi, his understanding of his mission grew, and simultaneously he developed friends who stood by him for the rest of his life.

Francis would rebuild the church at San Damiano and trust God with the rest. He sold all that he owned, including his horse, and gave the money to the church for distribution to the poor. He began begging for stones and building supplies in Assisi. He was moving from his life as a wealthy merchant's son to become a son of God who walked in the way of Jesus.

The changes in Francis were noticeable. He was no longer the playboy/knight wannabe. When he began wearing the clothes of the poor, the townspeople questioned his sanity. His father was incensed. Signore Bernardone had not worked for his wealth only to have it be given away to the poor—and by his own son!

Even after his family disowned him, Francis was not despondent. He chose a new family—the family of the poor. He felt God's presence and nudgings and continued sharing what he had with the poor. One by one people started coming to Francis, wanting to know more about the transformation they noticed. They were drawn by his kind acts toward others and his humble attitude. The wealthy merchant Bernard was the first to join Francis in his vow of poverty, but others—Egidio, Ruffino, and Leone—followed.

By the time Clare met Francis, the "Little Poor Men of God" had attracted quite a following. Like Francis, Clare had grown up among the elite. Unlike Francis, Clare had a long-standing reputation for being kind to the poor. It was this passion for the poor that drew Clare to Francis. Together with her cousin Pacifica, Clare left Assisi to join Francis and his brothers in their ministry. Francis and Clare would become close spiritual friends.

TRAITS OF FRIENDSHIP

Day 2 Exercise

READ PROVERBS 17:17; 19:6; AND ECCLESIASTES 4:9-10.

A friend loves at all times,
   and kinsfolk are born to share adversity.
—Proverbs 17:17

Many seek the favor of the generous,
   and everyone is a friend to a giver of gifts.—Proverbs 19:6

Two are better than one. . . . If they fall, one will lift up the other;
but woe to one who is alone and falls and does not have another to help.
—Ecclesiastes 4:9-10

REFLECT
- Who treats you like a friend "at all times" (Prov. 17:17), and who do you treat that way? Make a short list of "all-times friends."
- Who are your friends only when it benefits you or they "give gifts" (see Prov. 19:6)?
- Think back over the people you have come in contact with this week. Who left you with a sense of gratitude?

PRAY Give thanks for anyone this week who allowed you to express yourself or took time to listen and understand your perspective. Then ask God to show you individuals for whom you need to be such a friend, offering an open ear and heart.

ACT Stop and take time to actually listen to someone you greet or who greets you. Forget yourself for a few moments and just be interested in that person.

Day 2 Reading

It was a hot summer night on the busy streets of Rome—our group's first evening there, with a lot of excitement in the air. After a driving tour of the city and dinner together, we had free time to explore. Some went shopping; others went for gelato; some just sat on the Spanish Steps to people watch. James lingered.

A high school senior, James was one of the quieter members of the group. Everyone wished he would talk more. We could sense his depth and sincerity and commitment, but we didn't often get to hear what he was *really* thinking. That night, Jeanne, one of the trip leaders, invited James to join her on a casual stroll to the world-famous Trevi Fountain.

On their way to the fountain, Jeanne and James visited a church that was still open. They admired the architectural features and talked about the beauty of the city. By the time they arrived at the Trevi Fountain, it was almost time to head back to the Spanish Steps to meet up with the rest of the group.

Since Jeanne and James had known each other for a while, this was a pleasant time hanging out together. But in some extraordinary way, those ninety minutes were pivotal. Jeanne learned much about James's interests. She saw him light up when they talked about history and architecture. They laughed together and walked in silence together. Jeanne felt honored that the younger, quieter James shared more of himself with her. James felt honored and respected and accompanied by a trusted friend.

Their friendship today is deeper because of that grace-filled time. James attends college now, but when he is home, Jeanne is one of the people he seeks out. She is someone he can talk to easily, someone who shares in his joys and accomplishments.

THE PRACTICE OF BEING PRESENT

Day 3 Exercise

READ 2 SAMUEL 11:26–12:13.

I gave you your master's house, and your master's wives into your bosom, and gave you the house of Israel and of Judah; and if that had been too little, I would have added as much more. Why have you despised the word of the LORD, to do what is evil in his sight? You have struck down Uriah the Hittite with the sword, and have taken his wife to be your wife, and have killed him with the sword of the Ammonites.—2 Samuel 12:8-9

REFLECT The prophet Nathan demonstrates a prophetic dimension of friendship when he confronts King David with the truth about himself. Respectful listening to one another and to God can lead to deeper truthfulness. Are you struggling with whether to tell someone a hard truth? What could you learn from Nathan's motive and manner of "speaking the truth in love" (Eph. 4:15) to King David?

PRAY Take your situation to God in prayer and listen. Is the Lord sending you in love to speak, to listen, to pray, to learn more, or to confess and examine a hidden sin in your own life?

ACT Act in humility, love, and truth on what the Lord is sending you to do.

Day 3 Reading

Spiritual friends accompany one another, and accompaniment takes practice. Just ask any pianist who has ever had to play along with a singer. Or ask any basketball player who relies on a teammate for an assist. Where would Mick Jagger be without the Rolling Stones? It's easy to hang out together, but it takes practice to walk with another person so that we can anticipate that individual's responses and actions. To be in step with others without getting ahead of them or lagging behind takes practice—and grace.

So often our time with friends is consumed by doing things together—watching or playing sports, eating, going to the movies, maybe even going to church. But one of the gifts of spiritual friendships is that it doesn't matter so much what we do together. What really matters is how we are present to one another when we are together. Can we receive both encouragement and challenge from our friends?

The practice of accompaniment involves listening without having our own agenda. It means that I put my needs on hold so that I can really hear another. Deep listening is life-giving and perhaps one of the greatest gifts we can give our friends. Several decades ago, Catherine de Hueck Doherty said that listening offers the gift of healing to others and that it is possible even to "listen a person's soul into existence."[1]

SOUL FRIEND

Day 4 Exercise

READ RUTH 1:1-18.

> *But Ruth said,*
>   *"Do not press me to leave you or to turn back from following you!*
>   *Where you go, I will go;*
>   *Where you lodge, I will lodge;*
>   *your people shall be my people,*
>   *and your God my God."*—Ruth 1:16

REFLECT In the book of Ruth we read about Naomi, a woman whose husband and adult sons die. One daughter-in-law chooses not to leave Naomi but rather to go with her and be her companion. Ruth's words to Naomi (above) are the words of a "soul friend."

Who are your soul friends? Write in your journal the names of those individuals who help you be the best person you can be and who would stand by you through thick and thin.

PRAY Bring Christ, your everlasting soul friend, to mind. Speak the words of Ruth 1:16 (above) to him. Imagine Christ responding in kind. Have spiritual conversation with him about where this feels true and where you still need to work on your friendship.

ACT Be a soul friend to someone today, just as Christ is soul friend to you eternally.

Day 4 Reading

We have friends we go to movies with, friends we send birthday cards to, friends we camp or hike or play with. And there are some friends we let in deeper. We can have fun with our closest friends too, but our relationship with spiritual friends goes beyond recreation and common interests. These people are patient and loving enough to get to know us as we truly are.

Anam cara is a Gaelic term loosely translated "soul friend." It is often used to describe people who, though parted by miles or time, still maintain a connection deeply rooted in the work of the Spirit. Saints like Francis and Clare and even ordinary people like Jeanne and James are capable of these extraordinary friendships. Such friendships are the fruit of practiced presence and much grace.

When I was in seminary, four loosely connected friends and I retreated for a long weekend to a cabin in the mountains of North Carolina. It was rustic but comfortable. Our activity level was low. We took a couple of hikes but mostly napped, cooked meals, and sat by the fire. I remember one night we passed around a book of poetry by May Sarton and took turns reading poems we liked. I remember how easy it was to listen to one another. By the time the weekend ended, the five of us had formed a bond. I still feel that bond today and know that these four people are like family to me. They pray for me and are there for me, and I am for them. Each is *anam cara* to me.

LIFE-GIVING FRIENDSHIP

Day 5 Exercise

READ JOHN 15:12-17.

> *"This is my commandment, that you love one another as I have loved you. No one has greater love than this, to lay down one's life for one's friends."*—John 15:12-13

REFLECT In this passage, Jesus says to his disciples that they are no longer servants but friends. If Jesus had said this to you, how would you understand the difference between the two?

In light of Jesus' command "Love one another as I have loved you," reflect on your circle of friends in *The Way of Pilgrimage*. On a scale of 1 to 10 (1 being low, 10 being high), rate the quality of the love actually being shared and shown among you. After you have rated it, ask yourself what a higher rating would look like and what it would call for on your part.

PRAY Ask God to give you increased love for your friends. Ask God to show you what keeps you from loving more fully and how to remove those obstacles. Ask for love to be a friend to all whom God loves.

ACT As you walk through your day, listen for the Lord calling you to "love . . . as I have loved you."

Day 5 Reading

Some believe that the concept of *anam cara* developed from the relationship between two Irish monks. Saint Kevin and Saint Kieran were Irishmen who lived in the early sixth century. They came of age in a time when Christianity was rapidly expanding across Ireland. As young men dedicated to Christ, both spent extended periods of time in solitude, and both drew groups of people who wanted to learn from them and be blessed by them. Eventually Kevin established a monastic city in Glendalough, and Kieran founded a similar community at Clonmacnoise. These walled monastic cities were places of prayer, worship, healing, and hospitality for all the Irish people, including women and children.

Kevin and Kieran met and became close friends. Their friendship is recounted in much folklore across Ireland. In one account of their friendship, Kevin was walking from his home in Glendalough to the monastic city of Clonmacnoise to visit Kieran. But three days before Kevin arrived, Kieran became ill and died. The body was prepared and laid to rest in one of the churches in Clonmacnoise, so that the community could pay their respects. Kevin arrived late and entered the church where Kieran was laid. He asked everyone to leave so that he could be alone with his departed friend. Kevin was alone with the body of Kieran until the following day. But those waiting on the other side of the church doors reported hearing Kevin praying, and then they heard a conversation ensue between Kevin and Kieran. When Kevin emerged from the church, he was wearing the clothes of Kieran, and Kieran was wearing Kevin's clothes. The story tells us that Kieran's body was warm to the touch and that his face was flushed with life.[2]

Although this story may seem far-fetched, the fact that it has remained in Ireland's folklore for so long points to the value the Irish place on steadfast friendship. The story goes on to describe the sense of friendship that extended to the inhabitants of Glendalough and Clonmacnoise as a result of the friendship between Kevin and Kieran. Perhaps the fruit of their friendship is best seen in the lives they touched.

If you are an athlete, you need a good coach. If you are a musician, you appreciate a talented director. If you are a writer, you try to emulate the great writers of our time. And so as a disciple of Jesus Christ, you also want a mentor and guide in this journey. This week as you learn about the relationships of men and women who found guides and wise mentors in their lives, you will have time to identify such people in your own life.

MENTORING ONE ANOTHER

Day 1 Exercise

READ LUKE 1:39-45, 56.

> *When Elizabeth heard Mary's greeting, the child leaped in her womb. And Elizabeth was filled with the Holy Spirit and exclaimed with a loud cry, "Blessed are you among women, and blessed is the fruit of your womb." . . . And Mary remained with her about three months and then returned to her home.—Luke 1:41-42, 56*

REFLECT This is a story about a special mentoring relationship between young Mary, who was pregnant with Jesus, and her wise cousin Elizabeth, pregnant with John. What do you notice about the relationship between Elizabeth and Mary? What do you think Elizabeth did for Mary and vice versa? Why were those three months together important for them?

Think about people you can rely on for support, encouragement, and accountability. Who sees and celebrates the promise in your life? Who honors and respects what's happening inside you?

PRAY If you have an "Elizabeth" who has been a spiritual mentor, give thanks to God. If you don't, ask God to show you someone you may know, an adult, who would be honored to talk with you, share his or her life, and listen to what's happening in your life.

ACT Today look for the mature people around you. Which ones would you like to know more about and question about life?

Day 1 Reading

It is a gift to have true friends. But life is challenging, so we need trail guides as well. A trail guide participates less in our daily life than a friend but cares for us deeply nonetheless. Guides listen well to us and to the Spirit in order to help us see where the Spirit might be leading. Francis and Clare were friends, but because they were trailblazers in so many ways, they also served as guides for each other.

It didn't take long for Clare to gather a substantial following of godly young women who made vows of poverty, chastity, and obedience. Soon Bishop Guido saw the need to give the women a permanent residence in San Damiano, the very church that Francis had worked to restore. Unlike the system in other monasteries, here all the sisters were equal. They spent their days in prayer and humble service to one another.

Francis and Clare's followers lived similar lives in many ways. Both groups lived lives of poverty and depended on the generosity of others. Both prayed for the needs of others. But the social mores of thirteenth-century Italy did not permit single women and single men to join in ministry outside the walls of the church. As a result of that gender division, the communities developed two distinct ways of meeting the needs of the poor. Francis's group prayed and ministered directly to lepers and the indigent. In solidarity, Clare's community spent extended time in prayer, specifically remembering their Franciscan brothers and the poor to whom they ministered.

Over time, the movement Clare and Francis started strengthened. With recognition and increased numbers came new challenges and temptations. Often Francis and his followers went to Clare and her sisters for counsel, advice, and prayer. These two communities and their leaders, Francis and Clare, needed each other for accountability, support, and encouragement. Francis and Clare encouraged each other to recognize how God was present in their lives. As deep spiritual friends, they discerned together how God was calling them.

AFFIRMING ONE ANOTHER'S STRENGTHS

Day 2 Exercise

READ MATTHEW 16:13-18.

"And I tell you, you are Peter, and on this rock I will build my church, and the gates of Hades will not prevail against it."—Matthew 16:18

REFLECT In this story, we see Jesus doing what spiritual friends do for one another. Jesus nicknames Simon "Peter"—*petros*, which means "rock" in Greek. Though Peter had many weaknesses, Jesus saw greatness in him; Jesus saw a rock of a person, a rock of faith. In true Christian community, we likewise seek to see and name greatness in one another.

Jot down names of the members of your pilgrim group. What God-given strength or gift do you see in each of them? Try to find a metaphor from nature (an element, a geographic feature, an animal, a tree, or a flower, for instance) that somehow names and affirms what you see in these individuals.

PRAY Put yourself in the story with Jesus. Respond to Jesus' question "Who do you say I am?" Then listen as Jesus does for you what he did for Peter, naming the greatness he sees in you. Write what you hear in your journal.

ACT Seek to be a spiritual friend to someone today. Share with someone the greatness you see in him or her, especially someone who needs to hear it most.

Day 2 Reading

This past spring a dear friend of mine passed away. Father Francis, a Jesuit priest on staff at a retreat center about two hours from my home, had been my spiritual director for over six years. About four times a year I would plan meetings with Father Francis. I would make reservations to stay at the retreat house for two nights and meet with Father Francis for three hour-long sessions over the course of three days. The rest of the time I kept silence.

Although it wasn't long ago when I last met with Father Francis, I don't remember much that he said to me. Father Francis was a bright and wise man, but it was his character that I remember most. His kindheartedness and hospitality made an impression on me. Sometimes I would locate my room before meeting with him. Almost always I found a note from him welcoming me and simply inviting me into God's hospitality.

What strikes me most about my time with Father Francis is my sense that he fully expected and trusted my life was about to be transformed by God's love. He had great patience about this process and confidence in it as the work of grace. The word from God, he said, was "come." I simply needed to show up. I hope always to carry with me the belief he helped instill that God beckons me toward Love and that I don't have to do anything to earn or justify God's love for me.

Father Francis and I seldom corresponded between visits, but I knew he prayed for me. I will miss this man who so faithfully and lovingly accompanied me in my growth.

LISTENING BENEATH THE WORDS

Day 3 Exercise

READ JOHN 4:5-26.

The Samaritan woman said to him, "How is it that you, a Jew, ask a drink of me, a woman of Samaria?" (Jews do not share things in common with Samaritans.) Jesus answered her, "If you knew the gift of God, and who it is that is saying to you, 'Give me a drink,' you would have asked him, and he would have given you living water."—John 4:9-10

REFLECT In this story about Jesus' encounter with a Samaritan woman at a well, we see how, like a spiritual guide, he leads her to a deeper self-awareness and awareness of God's presence in her life.

Draw a picture of the well going deep down to a place where it connects with an underground stream of flowing water. As you reread the story, note where you see the woman "staying on the surface," "going deeper," and finally "reaching God's truth" in her exchange with Jesus. Mark these verses on your picture.

Where do you usually stay in your relationships and conversations? On your sketch, write names of people and places you associate with your experience of each level. Who or what encourages you get beneath surface talk to truth talk?

PRAY Place yourself at the well where Jesus met the woman. Jesus asked the woman for a drink to get the conversation started. What does Jesus ask you for? Listen. What do you hope he doesn't ask you about? Tell him.

ACT Today, commit some time to sitting and listening to someone. Listen for what's going on behind the words, in that person's spirit. Ask a question or two. Listen with love and pray for the person as you listen.

Day 3 Reading

"Spiritual direction" sounds like a heavy experience to me. I have never taken too well to authority, so being directed—especially in my spiritual life—does not appeal to me. Even so, I have found the relationship of spiritual direction life giving.

Here is how one writer describes this relationship:

> Spiritual direction is basically the guidance one Christian offers another to help that person "grow up in every way . . . into Christ" (Eph. 4:15). A spiritual guide is someone who can help us see and name our own experience of God. Each of us needs to grow out of a second-hand faith to a knowledge of the way the Spirit works in our lives.[1]

Another writer points out that spiritual directors listen to our life story "with an ear for the movement of the Holy, of the Divine."[2]

Spiritual direction is not therapy because it does not focus on analyzing or fixing a person's problems. Rather, spiritual direction involves inviting a spiritually mature person to help us hear God though the events of our life.

Traditionally, spiritual direction was considered a useful relationship for middle-aged adults with a strong sense of self and a desire to know God better. This perception is changing. Most of us, no matter what age, need assistance in perceiving God's word for us. Life experiences at any age require us to rethink our ideas of God and the world, so that the opportunity to hear God's call can be ongoing.

Spiritual guides can help us understand the language of God's love—both in God's universal message, which always reminds us that we are beloved, and in the way our belovedness is uniquely expressed through our gifts. In other words, spiritual directors facilitate our opening up in order to remember who we are and how we can live into our gifts. This process is important for people of faith, young or old.

BECOMING PEOPLE WITH SPIRITUAL EYES

Day 4 Exercise

READ 2 CORINTHIANS 5:16-17.

From now on, therefore, we regard no one from a human point of view; even though we once knew Christ from a human point of view, we know him no longer in that way. So if anyone is in Christ, there is a new creation: everything old has passed away; see, everything has become new!—2 Corinthians 5:16-17

REFLECT In this passage, we learn that as Christians we see "no one" from a merely human, external, superficial point of view, any more than we see Jesus Christ from a merely human point of view.

Every community has its "human point of view" for seeing and judging people, for sizing them up, putting them down, and assigning them to little boxes. What are some of the categories people use in your school or town? From a "human point of view" in your community, who would be judged nearer the top or the bottom?

PRAY Be "in Christ." View the people in these various categories through Christ's eyes. What do you see? What happens to the categories? View the people in your pilgrim group through Christ's eyes. What do you see differently?

ACT Memorize verse 16. Walk with it through the day as a reminder to stay "in Christ" and to see everyone through sacred eyes for as much of the day as you can.

Day 4 Reading

A fable is told about a group of elderly monks whose religious order was in decline. As the years passed, more and more of the brothers died, and no men were entering the community. Before long there were only five brothers left. Despondent and worried, the abbot decided to seek the advice of a rabbi who lived as a hermit in the woods.

The rabbi greeted the abbot warmly as if he were welcoming a long-lost friend. The two sipped tea by the fire. The fellowship was wonderful, but as dusk neared, the abbot knew he must leave. Before leaving he asked the rabbi, "Have you any words of advice or wisdom for me and my brothers?" The rabbi replied softly, "I have no advice; I can only tell you this one thing—that one of you is the Messiah."

Confused and curious, the abbot returned to the monastery and reported to the brothers what the rabbi had said. The brothers initially dismissed the thought, but as the days wore on, they could not get the rabbi's announcement out of their minds. The brothers started whispering in the hallway. "Do you think it might be Brother Michael?" "I noticed Brother Karl being especially kindhearted the other day." "What do you make of Brother Fred's increased interest in prayer lately?"

Before long the brothers began treating one another differently. After all, if Brother Fred or Karl or Michael were the Messiah, then they should listen to him and treat him with great respect.

When people from the village occasionally visited the monastery, they noticed a change in the way the brothers were treating one another. More joy and kindness and love were in evidence. Gradually people started coming to the monastery's services more often and brought friends. Before long there was a new candidate for the community, then another, then a third. In a few years, the monastery was once again filled with energetic and faithful followers of Christ.[3]

Like the rabbi in this story, a good spiritual guide helps us see situations in new ways. And a new perspective opens new doors to life.

FINDING A SPIRITUAL GUIDE

Day 5 Exercise

READ 1 SAMUEL 3:1-10.

Then Eli perceived that the LORD was calling the boy. Therefore Eli said to Samuel, "Go, lie down; and if he calls you, you shall say, "Speak, LORD, for your servant is listening."—1 Samuel 3:8b-9a

REFLECT In this familiar story we see old Eli serving as a spiritual guide, helping Samuel recognize the voice of the Lord in his experience. What experiences or background might have enabled Eli to serve as Samuel's spiritual guide and help him as he did?

If you could ask an "Eli" about your own questions and experiences, what would you ask? Whose wisdom do you trust with these questions?

PRAY Sit with Samuel's prayer: "Speak, Lord, for your servant is listening." With each breath you take, pray this prayer and listen for the Lord in the silence between breaths. You might want to let go of all words for a bit and simply listen. What comes to mind?

ACT If a possible "Eli" in your circle of acquaintances comes to mind, be bold and make a plan to contact him or her for "a few minutes just to ask a question or two."

Day 5 Reading

The relationship between Samuel and Eli in the first book of Samuel provides a biblical example of spiritual direction. Samuel's mother, Hannah, had not been able to conceive a child and had promised God that if she conceived a son, the child would be dedicated to God.

Hannah's son, Samuel, grew up in the shadow of the tabernacle as promised. He was mentored and instructed by the priest Eli. Scripture says, "And the boy Samuel grew up in the presence of the LORD," and "continued to grow both in stature and in favor with the LORD and with the people" (1 Sam. 2:21, 26). With the help of Eli, Samuel was learning the language of God's love.

Later, we read that the voice of God came to Samuel in the night. Each time Samuel heard God, he thought Eli was calling. At first, Eli assumed Samuel must be hearing things, but after the third call from God, Eli instructed Samuel to wait and listen to what the Lord was about to say. The Lord's words to Samuel were not favorable to the house of Eli. Even so, Eli knew that God was faithful and just. "It is the LORD; let him do what seems good to him" (1 Sam. 3:18).

Samuel continued to grow in favor with God, and the ministry and presence of Samuel became one of our tradition's great stories of faithfulness and love for God. In Samuel's parting words to the people, he instructs, "Serve [the LORD] faithfully with all your heart; for consider what great things he has done for you" (1 Sam. 12:24).

Samuel came to know God because of his mother's faithfulness and because of Eli's wisdom and kindness. Eli helped Samuel listen and hear God's unique call for his life.

This week you will start to reflect on the gift of a community of a faith. Your biblical ancestors, spiritual friends, and mentors are essential to a healthy and holistic understanding of God and Christian discipleship. Another aspect of your spiritual health is the community of friends that surround you on a regular basis. As you read the scriptures this week, keep in mind the groups of people (youth group, church, small group) that love you and hold you accountable.

WHERE DO YOU FIND COMMUNITY?

Day 1 Exercise

READ PSALM 133.

> *How very good and pleasant it is*
>   *when kindred live together in unity!*
>
> *It is like the dew of Hermon,*
>   *which falls on the mountains of Zion.*
> *For there the Lord ordained his blessing,*
> *life forevermore.—Psalm 133:1, 3*

REFLECT When have you experienced "how very good and pleasant it is when" friends click or a small group becomes a life-giving community of support and joy? When have you experienced the absence of such community—maybe a time when you felt isolated and lonely?

In your journal, draw circles to represent the groups of people that make up your life. Name them for their gift or role in your life. Try coloring them to represent your feeling about how life-giving or life-draining each is.

PRAY Close your eyes and ask the Spirit to bring to mind the persons in your life. As their faces come to mind, thank God for them, even those who are a challenge.

ACT As you encounter any of the people you prayed for, greet them in the spirit of God's love. Make visible the connection you made in prayer.

Day 1   Reading

Our society encourages independence and autonomy, so we can easily begin to believe that we can go it alone. When I take the Lone Ranger approach to life, it doesn't take me long to start losing my perspective. I begin to focus more on me and my needs and less on what is going on around me. I need faithful people to remind me of my interdependence with others. I also need the gift of others' perspectives on God, because I know that my glimpses of the Holy suggest only a partial picture of God's love. Francis and Clare needed this interaction too.

The followers of Francis and Clare grew in number partly because their reform movement was so timely. No one could have predicted the number of people who would be drawn to their way of life. Within ten years of Francis's departure from his family there were over three thousand Franciscans. Taking vows of poverty, chastity, and obedience, the Franciscans traveled throughout Europe as missionaries. They were interested in converting people to Christianity but also considered themselves reformers who challenged the church's wealth and misguided missions (such as the Crusades).

The Order of the Poor Clares remained cloistered at San Damiano with Clare as abbess. Although they never left the monastery grounds, word of their work and prayer life spread rapidly, and other monastic communities of women developed throughout Europe. A strong woman, Clare pushed the edges of expectations for women in the church. She refused to follow church guidelines for her daily life within the convent; instead, she fought for her own rule of life that would enable her community to remain connected to the church while not being financially dependent on it.

Francis and Clare's callings were difficult, but fortunately a small group of their closest friends encouraged them in their missions and helped hold them true to the calling God had given each one. Fulfilling relationships with like-minded companions enabled Francis and Clare to continue their meaningful ministry.

FINDING THE ZONE

Day 2 Exercise

READ MARK 6:30-32.

The apostles gathered around Jesus, and told him all that they had done and taught. He said to them, "Come away to a deserted place all by yourselves and rest a while." For many were coming and going, and they had no leisure even to eat. And they went away in the boat to a deserted place by themselves.—Mark 6:30-32

REFLECT These few verses provide insight into the cross-shaped pattern of life Jesus and his small group of disciples developed. After going out to do ministry in Jesus' name (the "horizontal" dimension), they would regather around Jesus, report and reflect on their experiences, and rest with Jesus in a quiet place before being sent out again (the "vertical" dimension). We might say this pattern put them "in the zone."

Draw a big cross and write the words *worship* and *devotion* at the top and bottom points, and the words *compassion* and *justice* at the two side points. Now draw a circle on the cross to represent the faith community, pilgrims meeting with one another on the Way. Reflect on where you participate (or could participate) in each of these aspects of the Christian life this week.

PRAY Close your eyes and visualize your day. Ask God to show you where you can make space for loving God in prayer and worship. Ask God to help you see where you can make space for loving people in acts of compassion and acts of justice. As you think of opportunities, write them on the cross at the appropriate points.

ACT When you meet with your *Way of Pilgrimage* group, report on your participation in this cross-shaped pattern of life.

Day 2 Reading

Late one Sunday night, after a hot day in Assisi of walking, reflecting, laughing, and eating great food, our St. Paul's pilgrim group gathered in the courtyard of our hospitality house to reflect on the day's events. There were funny stories, like the one Jacob told about the woman who helped him convert his cargo pants into shorts by zipping off the legs. And there were questions about the mystery meat in our bag lunch. We also talked of meeting helpful people in the market and of the new flavors of gelato we sampled that day.

As the stories continued, we sensed that our spirits were moving like a spiral or labyrinth to a deep center. All the stories—even the funny ones—felt sacred, and with each chuckle we seemed to enter deeper into the mystery of God's love. Particular stories directly addressed mystery, like the worship service we witnessed in the chapel where Saint Francis is buried. The cavelike structure was completely packed with worshipers and pilgrims. Although we could not understand the words of the liturgy, our familiarity with the form allowed us to follow along. Several of us had a goose-bumps experience—as if we were standing on holy ground.

As we spoke and listened, our time of sharing was rich with a sense of timelessness. Our group had found "the zone." We were experiencing pilgrimage. Before, *pilgrimage* had simply been a heady concept to us. Now, no longer tourists, we were graced to be pilgrims on holy ground, seeking the sacred center of God's love—in the lives of Clare and Francis and in one another's lives. We were depending on and learning from one another.

BEING CHRIST FOR ONE ANOTHER

Day 3 Exercise

READ JOHN 11:17-44.

Then Jesus, again greatly disturbed, came to the tomb. It was a cave, and a stone was lying against it. . . . "Lazarus, come out!" The dead man came out, his hands and feet bound with strips of cloth, and his face wrapped in a cloth. . . . Jesus said to them, "Unbind him, and let him go."—John 11:38, 43b-44

REFLECT The story of Lazarus illustrates Jesus' way of inviting the community of faith to cooperate with God's resurrection power.

Ponder Jesus' three requests for the disciples' cooperation: "Take away the stone"; "Unbind him"; and "Let him go." Reread verses 38-44 and meditate on how Christ can work through spiritual friends today to accomplish similar actions.

PRAY
- Is Christ calling you to help "take away the stone" that keeps someone down or entombed in an old way of life? Ask Christ how you can assist that person.
- Who is Christ calling you to "unbind" from external wrappings or unhealthy attachments? Again, ask for guidance.
- Who is Christ calling you to "let go," to free for new life? Ask for strength and insight.

ACT Be the spiritual friend Christ is calling you to be for someone today.

Day 3   Reading

Why does it matter if we are connected to others or to a small group? After all, we live in a culture where we are able to fend for ourselves; independence is considered a virtue. Just do it—right?

People of faith need other people of faith to encourage and remind them that they are not alone and that God is with them. If physical isolation can lead to disorientation and depression in a matter of days, doesn't it make sense that people can also become disoriented spiritually?

Our culture tells us that what matters is how we look, what we wear, what we drive, and what school we attend. But small groups of faithful traveling companions can reorient us and remind us that we are deeply loved; we don't have to prove our worth. Our pilgrimage together leads to knowing not only our belovedness but also our purpose. And that we are not alone!

In order for our faith to grow, we need to be around people who encourage us and hold us accountable for our actions. Some of us find such support in Sunday school classes or Bible study groups. Other places to find faithful friends are online support networks, twelve-step groups that deal with addictions, and organizations like Fellowship of Christian Athletes or campus ministry groups.

We need one another for survival because by ourselves we are only one part of the body of Christ. Being surrounded by Christians with different gifts, abilities, and ideas fosters better understanding of Jesus' life and mission. Alone, we have only piece of the picture; we need others to help us fill in the gaps of how God's love is taking shape in the world.

WATCHING AND WAITING TOGETHER

Day 4 Exercise

READ ACTS 11:25-30; 13:1-3.

Then Barnabas went to Tarsus to look for Saul, and when he had found him, he brought him to Antioch. So it was that for an entire year they met with the church and taught a great many people, and it was in Antioch that the disciples were first called "Christians."—Acts 11:25-26

REFLECT These and similar episodes in Acts show us the way Paul, Barnabas, and their fellow missioners worked together in spiritual community. The practice of listening to the Spirit's leading was central to their manner of meeting and moving.

Consider your life in the Spirit. With whom do you (or could you) listen to the guidance of the Spirit for your lives or for next steps as a group? How would you or a group do that together? Write your thoughts.

PRAY Take a few minutes now to identify, with the Spirit's guidance, a specific issue or decision on your mind. Voice the central question you are struggling with and record it in your journal. Stay open to any stirring of the Spirit regarding your struggle.

ACT Ask three or four trusted friends to meet with you to help you listen to the Spirit. Allow them to pray for you, hear your question, and ask you questions that will assist you to find your way in the light of Christ. If the way forward is still not clear, ask your friends to hold you in prayer and set a time to meet again.

Day 4 Reading

Their friendship and their religious communities enabled Francis and Clare to hear God's word and will more clearly. The Franciscans and the Poor Clares developed out of the call these two young adults felt to serve the poor and to pray. Their religious communities—or orders—reminded their founders of this call and held them accountable to continue the mission. Even so, the two friends were tempted to lose sight of God's love and provision. Clare and Francis needed each other and their closest friends for mutual prayer, direction, support, and camaraderie.

You do not have to go far from home on a pilgrimage to make a monumental difference in the world. Simply being you is enough. Living into your belovedness despite all the voices that tell you otherwise will be a tremendous pilgrimage full of many adventures. But you will need faithful companions for this journey.

It is never too early to pray about your life and to find a small group of friends to provide you with support and encouragement. The group may already be in front of you. Maybe your group consists of other volunteers at the hospital where you work. Perhaps the group is composed of fellow camp counselors from last summer. Maybe it is your buddies from the soccer team. Or maybe the group that will support you and your dreams is one that you will have to pull together. You might agree to have Bible study together, pray together, or simply come together around a weekly meal.

It doesn't matter so much what the composition of the group is or what you do when you come together. What matters most is that you agree to be attentive to one another and to the work of the Spirit in your lives. Like pilgrims around a campfire, watch and wait together for God to speak a loving word to you and your group; then support one another as you forge ahead.

STAYING AT THE TABLE

Day 5 Exercise

READ MARK 14:17-25.

> *When it was evening, he came with the twelve. And when they had taken their places and were eating, Jesus said, "Truly I tell you, one of you will betray me, one who is eating with me."—Mark 14:17-18*

REFLECT The story of the Last Supper illustrates that community without conflict is an illusion; conflict and communion go hand in hand. The glory of Jesus' communion with his disciples is not that all was harmonious but that Jesus stayed at the table in self-giving love despite the betrayal, denial, and eventual abandonment he knew would come.

What real or potential conflicts threaten to hurt your church, youth group, or *Way of Pilgrimage* group? What does it mean to "stay at the table" with one another in the forgiving spirit of Christ despite the pain that you can cause each other?

PRAY Picture your group sitting at table with Jesus and his staying with you despite your conflicts. Open your heart to what Jesus wants to say and what he wants to give to you and your group.

ACT If you believe you have sinned or hurt another, go acknowledge it and ask that person's forgiveness. If someone has sinned against you or hurt you, go to that individual in forgiving love and make a good-faith effort to work through the difficulty.*

*EXCEPTION: If someone older than you has seriously hurt you through physical or emotional abuse, do not try this exercise by yourself. Get some good counsel from a mature and wise adult; approach an abuser only with a strong advocate present.

Day 5 Reading

Even Jesus needed traveling companions, so he summoned twelve men who showed potential for ministry and for sharing his vision of God's peaceable kingdom. The Bible indicates that "Jesus summoned his twelve disciples and gave them authority over unclean spirits, to cast them out, and to cure every disease and every sickness" (Matt. 10:1). Along with the Twelve, Mary, Martha, Mary Magdalene, and other women were also close followers of Jesus.

The writer of Matthew refers to Judas as the one who betrayed Jesus, but in many ways each apostle let Jesus down. One denied him; one doubted his claim of resurrection; some expressed disbelief when he asked them to participate with him in miracles; and then there were the feuding few who jockeyed for power and prestige among the group.

With traveling companions like these, who needs enemies? So if it wasn't complete loyalty, perfect humility, or steadfast faith that Jesus sought in his small group, what was it? What did Jesus see in these disciples that caused him to invite them along on his pilgrimage? Perhaps he knew that becoming faithful, loyal, and humble was a journey in itself. Even if these twelve weren't perfect, no doubt they had hidden qualities that would outlast their fickleness.

As it turns out, tradition tells us that perhaps nine of the twelve were martyred for the sake of Jesus' vision. And the women consistently stood by Jesus in his life on earth and afterward. Jesus may have sensed their hidden loyalty, or he may simply have known that people are capable of both great and awful things. He also knew the gift of the Holy Spirit eventually would strengthen them.

This part of our story reminds us that our pilgrimage team will let us down from time to time (and we them). That doesn't mean we should abandon them but rather recommit ourselves to our call and our openness to God's Spirit. We need others, and they need us!

Close friends and an intimate community of faith are incredible gifts from God. But they can also become too comfortable, encouraging us to hang out only with people who look, act, talk, and think like we do. Jesus was never happy hanging out with the "in crowd." He constantly challenged his circle of friends to grow larger and include more people, especially those that the world had abandoned. Allow your reading and prayers this week to open your eyes to persons who need the same invitation and friendship that has been offered to you through Jesus Christ.

BEFRIENDING THE LEPER

Day 1   Exercise

READ LUKE 5:12-16.

> *Once, when he was in one of the cities, there was a man covered with leprosy. When he saw Jesus, he bowed with his face to the ground and begged him, "Lord, if you choose, you can make me clean." Then Jesus stretched out his hand, touched him, and said, "I do choose. Be made clean." Immediately the leprosy left him.*—Luke 5:12-13

REFLECT Jesus befriended not only disciples but those who were otherwise outcasts, in this case a leper. Though the law prohibited lepers from interacting with "normal" people, and vice versa, Jesus jumped the boundary; he reached out to touch with healing love.

Who are "lepers" in your town, school, or church—people who suffer isolation? What fears keep you from being with them? Record those fears in your journal. Picture what it would mean to jump the gap and connect with these individuals as human beings.

PRAY Visualize Jesus stretching out his hand and touching someone regarded as a leper in your world. Ask Jesus to help you stretch out your hand and do likewise.

ACT Turn the stretching exercise you began in prayer into some kind of action today.

Day 1 Reading

When Francis first came to know God, he was a young man in his father's home. Early on, Francis knew God was speaking to him and that his life was about to change—he just didn't know how much.

Francis had always been repulsed by the lepers who suffered in isolation outside the city walls. They often begged for money and food; and whenever Francis encountered lepers, he hurried by them as quickly as possible, repelled by their appearance and stench.

One day Francis was traveling back to Assisi when he was startled by a leper asking for money. His first impulse was to hurry past the man, but in his heart he heard the words, "'What you used to abhor shall be to you joy and sweetness,'. . . and with a mighty victory over himself, Francis sprang from his horse, approached the leper, . . . placed his alms in the outstretched wasted hand—bent down quickly and kissed the fingers of the sick man."[1] Once Francis was back on his horse, he felt as if the whole event had been a dream and could barely remember how he had managed to mount the horse. He was deeply excited and felt a joy in his soul that he had never known.

Francis did not heal the leper or solve his financial woes. Francis did not fix the social structures that kept the man in an isolated camp outside the city. But for this brief moment, Francis practiced accompanying the poor. His act must have had impact on the leprous man. And this "chance" meeting gave new life to Francis as well. From that point on, Francis intuitively knew that part of his pilgrimage must include time and presence with the marginalized of his society.

THE GIFT OF ACCOMPANIMENT

Day 2 Exercise

READ MARK 10:13-16.

But when Jesus saw this, he was indignant and said to them, "Let the little children come to me; do not stop them; for it is to such as these that the kingdom of God belongs."—Mark 10:14

REFLECT Contrary to customs that dictated how children should pay respect to holy men, Jesus welcomed the children and blessed them. Notice how Jesus was "indignant" with those who tried to keep the children from coming to him. Who gets between children and God's welcoming love in your community? With whom would Jesus be indignant?

PRAY Where have you seen children this week? Imagine them running into Jesus' arms. Let him receive them and bless them. Then imagine being the arms and hands of Jesus as he "took them up in his arms, laid his hands on them, and blessed them."

ACT When you see children today, no matter how dirty or clean, seek a way to be Christ's "arms" to them.

Day 2 Reading

Simply being with a person who is marginalized can be a radical and transforming experience. Two years ago a group of young people from my church felt a call to start a mission project that they could continue on an ongoing basis. After some research and prayer, they decided that they wanted to work with sick children. We invited the pediatric chaplain from our local research hospital to come talk to us about the possibility.

We learned that because of security concerns, we would not be able to ask the children anything about their personal lives. We would only know their first names. We also could not ask them anything about their illnesses. The chaplain told us that some of the children might die. She wanted to prepare us for this possibility to make sure that we knew what we were about to jump into. After more prayer and discussion, the group decided to proceed.

The young people quickly learned the gift of accompaniment. There was not much they could do to help the children, but they came to see their presence with and attention to the children as healing. They visited the children regularly. It seemed that no matter what the young people faced there, they always left the hospital with a fresh perspective about what really matters in life. Their time with the kids gave them joy.

In Matthew 18:1-5, we read:

> At that time the disciples came to Jesus and asked, "Who is the greatest in the kingdom of heaven?" He called a child, whom he put among them, and said, "Truly I tell you, unless you change and become like children, you will never enter the kingdom of heaven. Whoever becomes humble like this child is the greatest in the kingdom of heaven. Whoever welcomes one such child in my name welcomes me."

Jesus wants our pilgrimage to be joyful and open to all . . . especially the "least of these" (Matt. 25:40).

A SAFE AND SAVING HELP

Day 3 Exercise

READ GENESIS 6:13-21.

"But I will establish my covenant with you; and you shall come into the ark, you, your sons, your wife, and your sons' wives with you."—Genesis 6:18

REFLECT Noah's ark often serves as an image of a safe, saving place to be and grow in the midst of a dangerous, death-dealing world.

Imagine your youth group or campus group as a safe and saving place like Noah's ark. Where does this community require and demonstrate genuine acceptance, patience, and companionship? Where do you see transformation?

PRAY Ask God to show you who within your reach could benefit from being welcomed onto this ark. Open your heart as fully as you can to the wideness of God's grace.

ACT Let Christ reach out and touch a struggling soul today through you.

Day 3 Reading

In 1964 at the age of thirty-six, Jean Vanier, together with Father Thomas Philippe, founded the first L'Arche community in Trosly-Breuil, France. *L'Arche* means "the ark" in French. L'Arche communities were created to welcome people with a mental handicap. It was the hope of L'Arche "to respond to the distress of those who are too often rejected, and to give them a valid place in society."[2] The first act by Vanier and Philippe was to invite two men with mental disabilities to join them in this community.

Since the first L'Arche community began, over one hundred other communities have been established around the world. "These communities, called into being by God, are united by the same vision and the same spirit of welcome, of sharing and simplicity."[3] Being a welcoming place for people with mental disabilities sounds very Franciscan—a choice out of faith in God to be with those who are poor, neglected, and marginalized. It also sounds a lot like Jesus' life and ministry. The more you learn about L'Arche, the more you see these communities fleshing out Jesus' sense of the belovedness of all human beings.

A friend who lived at L'Arche in Canada tells of the patience it takes to live among people with severe physical and mental challenges. But he also shares stories of personal transformation and of great joy. Author, priest, and teacher Henri Nouwen, who spent time at L'Arche in Canada, wrote about his encounter there with Adam:

> After a month of working with Adam, something started to happen to me that had never happened before. This severely handicapped young man whom outsiders sometimes describe with very hurtful words started to become my dearest companion. As I carried him into his bath and made waves to let the water run fast around him and told him all sorts of stories, I knew that two friends were communicating far beyond the realm of thought.
>
> Before this I had come to believe that what makes us human is our minds, but Adam keeps showing me that what makes us human is our heart, the center of our being where God has hidden trust, hope and love.[4]

ACCEPTING THE MARYS AND THE MARTHAS

Day 4 Exercise

READ LUKE 10:38-42.

Now as they went on their way, he entered a certain village, where a woman named Martha welcomed him into her home. She had a sister named Mary, who sat at the Lord's feet and listened to what he was saying.—Luke 10:38-39

REFLECT Mary and Martha often serve to illustrate two kinds of people who make up Christian community, and the need for both: those more inclined to serve Jesus through listening and prayer and those inclined to serve Jesus through action.

Make two columns on a piece of paper, one labeled "Mary" and one "Martha." Think about the people in your *Way of Pilgrimage* group. Write the names of those who are more like Mary under her name and those with characteristics like Martha under her name. How do they offer a balanced ministry when taken together? What do the Marys and the Marthas add to your group's overall experience?

PRAY Pray with Mary by sitting at the Lord's feet and listening to what he wants to say for a few minutes. What is his message for you today? What call do you hear?

Pray with Martha by telling the Lord all that troubles you about your serving and the people with whom you serve. Then listen to what he wants you to hear.

ACT Live out what your Mary side hears with the energy of Martha. Act on what the Lord calls you to do.

Day 4 Reading

In Luke 10:38-42 we read a story of two women who care deeply for Jesus, both of whom are excited about the prospect of offering Jesus hospitality in their home. The passage reads:

> Now as they went on their way, he entered a certain village, where a woman named Martha welcomed him into her home. She had a sister named Mary, who sat at the Lord's feet and listened to what he was saying. But Martha was distracted by her many tasks; so she came to him and asked, "Lord, do you not care that my sister has left me to do all the work by myself? Tell her then to help me." But the Lord answered her, "Martha, Martha, you are worried and distracted by many things; there is need of only one thing. Mary has chosen the better part, which will not be taken away from her."

This story frustrates those of us who are doers. We want to make sure that everyone is cared for and that the party doesn't flop. We want to know that when the guests look back on the event, people remember a good time. Although this desire is noble, Jesus seems instead to place the emphasis on simply being together.

Mary is the kind of person who might frustrate us if we are in charge of a party. But Mary is so delighted to have Jesus in her home that nothing else matters to her except sitting in Jesus' presence. She doesn't want to miss a moment of the opportunity, and so lingers at his feet, hanging on his every word and relishing his presence. Mary teaches us that sometimes just being with someone is enough. And Jesus commends her choice.

BEING WITH THE LEAST AND THE LAST

Day 5 Exercise

READ MATTHEW 25:31-46.

> *"Come, you that are blessed by my Father, inherit the kingdom prepared for you from the foundation of the world; for I was hungry and you gave me food, I was thirsty and you gave me something to drink, I was a stranger and you welcomed me, I was naked and you gave me clothing, I was sick and you took care of me, I was in prison and you visited me."—Matthew 25:34b-36*

REFLECT This passage, often called the parable about the final judgment, is also a parable about what it means to be in community with Jesus and his friends.

Notice who needs whom in this parable. How does being in relationship with the least and the last bring you into deeper relationship with Jesus? Identify one real place where you could go today to encounter Jesus in your service to others.

PRAY Reread verses 37-39 or verse 44 as though this were your personal question to the Lord: "When did I see you . . . ?" Then listen prayerfully for how the Lord answers you.

ACT Make a trip to the place you identified in your reflection time. Go meet Jesus in your service to someone there today.

Day 5 Reading

Jesus tells us in Matthew 25 that if we treat the "least of these" with kindness, it is as if we are kind to him too. He goes on to say that when we do this, the kingdom of heaven is ours. Why is this so important to Jesus? What does this mean for our pilgrimage?

It is all part of Jesus' upside-down thinking. He tells us that the first shall be last and the last shall be first. He tells us that in giving everything away we will find true wealth. He seems to want us to travel on this pilgrimage with a vast array of friends, including those the world tells us will only slow us down. But for Jesus, the destination is determined by the character of the journey. *Who we become as we journey together is more important than reaching our worldly goals.*

Jean Vanier says:

We will never win the Olympics of humanity, racing for perfection, but we can walk together in hope, celebrating that we are loved in our brokenness, helping each other, growing in trust, living in thanksgiving, learning to forgive, opening up to others, welcoming them, and striving to bring peace and hope to our world. So it is that we come to put down roots in community—not because it is perfect and wonderful, but because we believe that Jesus has called us together. It is where we belong, and are called to grow and serve.[5]

When we accompany people on the margins, we help them remember their God-given belovedness. They in turn remind us of our belovedness by pointing us past all the superficial things we think make us who we are. We are blessed already. We just need one another to keep us mindful of that fact. Then we can all journey together joyfully and with purpose.

You have chosen to participate in this group designed to strengthen your relationship with God and to form you in the image of Christ. So you already understand the importance of finding traveling companions. It takes time to seek out these spiritual friendships and to build community. This week prayerfully remember the individuals who have traveled these six weeks with you.

HELPING US GROW IN LOVE

Day 1   Exercise

READ EPHESIANS 3:14-19.

> *I pray that you may have the power to comprehend, with all the saints, what is the breadth and length and height and depth, and to know the love of Christ that surpasses knowledge, so that you may be filled with all the fullness of God.—Ephesians 3:18-19*

REFLECT Begin writing a list of all the people, both living and dead, whose lives reflect Christ's love and who you would like to have as spiritual companions on your pilgrimage.

PRAY Ask God to show you more people whose lives and witness will encourage your growth in love.

ACT Circle two to four names of living people on the list of saints you are making. Will you find some way to let them know how you value their life and influence?

Day 1 Reading

In the best of all worlds our pilgrimage through life will include all kinds of interesting and Spirit-filled people. Those who have gone before us can instruct us and assist us to grow in love and joy. There are everyday saints—both living and dead—who instruct me. I have pleasant dreams about my grandmother who died about eight years ago. I hear her laughter and remember her tender presence and know that her loving influence and positive outlook will always be with me.

Then there are the church's saints like Francis and Clare who continue to teach me. Walking the streets and paths of Assisi, I had a real sense that something important happened there. I wanted to linger in that hilltop town and take it all in and learn more. In the sparseness and diligence of their poverty and prayer, the lives of these two saints overflowed with love and joy.

In "The Canticle of the Sun," Francis wrote:

Be praised, my Lord, through all your creatures, especially through my lord Brother Sun, who brings the day; and you give light through him. And he is beautiful and radiant in all his splendor! Of you, Most High, he bears the likeness.

Be praised, my Lord, through Sister Moon and the stars; in the heavens you have made them, precious and beautiful. . . .

Be praised, my Lord, through our sister Mother Earth, who feeds us and rules us, and produces various fruits with colored flowers and herbs.[1]

These are not the words of a pinched ascetic who endured hardship as a martyr. These are the songs of a man who once lived the life of the rich and famous and then discovered a better way—a pilgrimage toward joyful union with God. I want to absorb the joy and love Francis and Clare knew and intend to seek their continued company as mentors of my soul.

HELPING EACH OTHER MATURE IN CHRIST

Day 2 Exercise

READ COLOSSIANS 1:24-29.

It is he whom we proclaim, warning everyone and teaching everyone in all wisdom, so that we may present everyone mature in Christ. For this I toil and struggle with all the energy that he powerfully inspires within me.—Colossians 1:28-29

REFLECT This passage describes the heart of the faith community's purpose and promise.

Consider what you and your friends "toil and struggle" for as believers. What does "mature in Christ" look like for you, for a group, for a faith community?

PRAY Ask God for one insight into how your group can encourage and facilitate one another's spiritual growth.

ACT Act on the insight God gives you. Prepare to share it with your group at the next meeting.

Day 2 Reading

Along with the saints, peers and friends can also be faithful companions on the pilgrimage. They share our interests and concerns and know us—warts and all. Because they know us, they can help us mature in Christ. One or more of them may become our soul friends (*anam caras*). True friends recognize our belovedness even when we can't see it ourselves; they remind us who we truly are in a culture that tells us we have to measure up to arbitrary and external standards.

Elders, spiritual guides, and spiritual directors are significant too. These are people, usually outside our everyday interactions, who listen to our soul. They pray with us and help us tune our ears to God's word for us.

Small groups of faithful companions are also critical for growth in Christ. A group prevents our becoming isolated from the faith story and keeps our focus on the parts of life that matter most. A small group can bring our attention back to our gifts and our limitations as well as open us to learning from the gifts of others. We are the body of Christ and need one another to gain a clearer understanding of who God is and how God's love gets fleshed out in the world.

Finally, we cannot fully mature in Christ without learning to walk with people on the margins of society. As we have learned from Saint Francis and others, relationships with those the world rejects teach us who Jesus really is and what is important to him. These relationships promise both joy and authentic transformation of our hearts and lives.

FANNING THE FLAME OF FAITH

Day 3   Exercise

READ 2 TIMOTHY 1:3-7.

For this reason I remind you to rekindle the gift of God that is within you through the laying on of my hands; for God did not give us a spirit of cowardice, but rather a spirit of power and of love and of self-discipline.—2 Timothy 1:6-7

REFLECT   This letter reminds young Timothy to remember the faith of his grandmother and mother and to "rekindle the gift" (literally "to fan the flame") of God within him. Here we find another image illustrating the purpose of Christian community: to fan the flames of faith in one another.

What is the gift of God within you? Draw a flame. Beside the flame write words naming the deep desires and dreams that burn within you. Also name people whose memory, ministry, or friendship rekindles those yearnings in you.

PRAY   Offer your deepest dreams and desires to God. Listen for how the Spirit may respond in your heart.

ACT   Fan the flames of faith in someone else today. Call a person in your group to share the gift of God within you, and ask that person also to share the gift within.

Day 3 Reading

What is the purpose of this grand pilgrimage? Why not just go to school or work and hang out with our friends? Why not fill our lives with entertainment, stuff, and all that the world says we need to succeed? If this pilgrimage requires saints, friends, small groups, and the marginalized to go along with us, is the trip really worth it? The answer to this question depends on whether you want just life or Life.

Unlike an actual journey to Assisi, Rome, or Jerusalem, a pilgrimage of the spirit takes us inward as well as outward to the vast terrain of God's reality. This pilgrimage puts us in touch with our deepest desires. All human beings face the profound yearning to belong and to know we are accepted. Joining the company of other pilgrims assures us of communities where we can experience our belovedness and belonging.

As we grow into our sense of being Jesus' beloved brothers and sisters, we come to trust the deep yearnings of our heart to follow him. We come to believe that these desires are God-given even if they don't make sense to others. Such desires can become the road map for our pilgrimage. Elizabeth O'Connor writes:

> In our wishes, small urgings, dreams, and fantasies, we are given intimations of the way we are to go. It is our way alone and cannot be learned by reading books or listening to scholars or following others. We can learn our way only by taking seriously the sign that we see and the small voice that we hear. These we must treasure up in our hearts and ponder over. The code we are to decipher is written into our genes and sent out to us, as it were, from the core of our beings.[2]

Even if our personal road map is sketchy, faithful companions assist us in filling out the picture. They encourage us to identify our deepest desires and dreams so we may gradually discover our unique path in life and unique gifts for serving God.

STRENGTHENING THE COMMUNITY

Day 4 Exercise

READ ACTS 2:42-47; 4:32-34.

There was not a needy person among them, for as many as owned lands or houses sold them and brought the proceeds of what was sold.
—Acts 4:34

REFLECT This description of the early church highlights distinctive marks of Christian communities: teaching and fellowship, breaking of bread and prayers, and sharing of all they possessed.

Think about your church in light of these marks of Christian community. In which areas do you see strength? Which need strengthening?

Reread the passage. What elements of this vision attract you? What scares or repels you? Note key thoughts in your journal.

PRAY Ask God for release from fear that prevents greater generosity in sharing yourself and your possessions for the sake of Christ's community. Praise God for the grace that is already evident in your community.

ACT Identify at least one gift you can offer to strengthen your Christian community and offer it.

Day 4 Reading

The early church we read about in Acts may offer the best example of what it means to be in communion with others as we journey through life. In Acts 2 we get a glimpse of the early days of faith for those living in the very recent light of Jesus' resurrection. We read about the coming of the Holy Spirit, when those gathered in Jerusalem for the Jewish celebration of Pentecost were able to hear the story of Jesus in their own languages. Peter preached to the crowd, and thousands came to believe Jesus was indeed God's Messiah.

But here is the real miracle. After Pentecost believers came together and lived in such a way that others were attracted to their way of life and wanted to know their secret. Here's how the Bible describes it in Acts 2:42-47:

> They devoted themselves to the apostles' teaching and fellowship, to the breaking of bread and the prayers.
>
> Awe came upon everyone, because many wonders and signs were being done by the apostles. All who believed were together and had all things in common; they would sell their possessions and goods and distribute the proceeds to all, as any had need. Day by day, as they spent much time together in the temple, they broke bread at home and ate their food with glad and generous hearts, praising God and having the goodwill of all the people. And day by day the Lord added to their number those who were being saved.

Early on, Christians were known simply as "people of the way," the way of Jesus. The people of the way were pilgrim people, and they traveled together as friends, saints, and guides. They journeyed into the unknown by the grace of the Spirit one step at a time, and other people followed them because they recognized spiritual power and freedom in this pilgrim community.

AN OASIS IN THE DESERT

Day 5 Exercise

READ ISAIAH 35:1-10.

The wilderness and the dry land shall be glad, the desert shall rejoice and blossom; like the crocus it shall blossom abundantly, and rejoice with joy and singing.—Isaiah 35:1-2a

REFLECT In this passage the prophet Isaiah describes a God-given vision for the future, despite hard times and the fact that the kingdoms of Israel and Judah are under threat.

Which verses from the passage speak most powerfully to you?

Draw an image that represents a vision of the promise of life God is nurturing in you. Then write a few sentences that describe what the image means to you.

PRAY Let the passage speak to you and listen for God's call to you through its verses. Ask God for strength to become the vision you pray for.

ACT Find one way to act on a verse that grasps you.

Day 5 Reading

Imagine walking across a hot desert. You are parched, dirty, tired. The sun bears down; you are out of food; and your water supply is dwindling. With nothing but sand dunes in every direction, what was an adventure has turned into sheer survival. You wonder how long you can continue. The promise of good times, riches, and hidden treasure seems far away.

Climbing a dune, you stumble. But as you near the top, you see a plume of smoke on the horizon. Your greatest hope is realized. Half a mile away lies an oasis. A spring in the desert has produced green vegetation, and the smoke carries the smell of food. You are not alone.

As you near the oasis, you hear sounds of laughter and music. Children race to greet you and assist you with your backpack. You drop to your knees on the grassy stream bank and lap up cool water. As you raise your head, you are greeted by people who help you up.

For the next few days you recuperate in the company of your new friends. There are young people and old, people of different races and physical abilities—everyone is welcomed and celebrated. When a new person comes from the desert, the pilgrims express great joy. You wonder if this is the treasure you were meant to find.

One day the group decides to leave the oasis. A sense of joyful adventure and confidence pervades the group as you all head out. Together you will find a way across the desert, and together you will not only survive but thrive. The sound of children laughing and wind whispering in your ears warms your soul. You look up at the blue sky and notice a beautiful pink cloud ahead, a reminder of God's grace and presence.

This image of desert and oasis, while it may strike you as a bit utopian, points to an image of God's reign on earth that challenges us to embrace interdependence over independence, celebration over despair, belonging over exclusion, and belovedness over meritocracy.

Ever since we took our first breath, we have been on a pilgrimage. We started out as God's beloved children, and we are still loved by God, no matter what path we are on. We are invited to look for the image of God in all those we pass on our way, and we are invited to choose and bless our faithful traveling companions. The risen Christ will continue to guide us until, together, we come home to the very heart of God.

NOTES

WEEK TWO

1. Catherine de Hueck Doherty, *Poustinia: Christian Spirituality of the East for Western Man* (Notre Dame, Ind.: Ave Maria Press, 1975), 161.

2. John O'Hanlon, *Lives of the Irish Saints*, vol. 6 (Dublin: James Duffy and Sons, 1891).

WEEK THREE

1. Marjorie J. Thompson, *Soul Feast: An Invitation to the Spiritual Life* (Louisville, Ky.: Westminster/John Knox Press, 1995, 2005), 103–4.

2. Jeffrey S. Gaines as quoted on Spiritual Directors International Web site: http://sdiworld.org/index.pl/what_is_spiritual_direction2.html; see topic "What Is Christian Spiritual Direction?"

3. Condensed and paraphrased from M. Scott Peck, "Prologue to The Rabbi's Gift," in *The Different Drum: Community-Making and Peace* (New York: Touchstone, 1998), 13–15.

WEEK FIVE

1. Johannes Jörgensen, *St. Francis of Assisi* (New York: Image Books, 1955), 38, 39.

2. http://www.larchecanada.org/charter1.htm

3. Ibid.

4. Henri J. M. Nouwen, as quoted on "Speaking of Faith," National Public Radio, http://speakingoffaith.publicradio.org/programs/larche/particulars.shtml; based on a passage from Nouwen's book *Adam: God's Beloved* (Maryknoll, N.Y.: Orbis Books, 1997).

5. Jean Vanier, *The Broken Body: Journey to Wholeness* (Toronto: Anglican Book Centre, 1988), 99.

WEEK SIX

1. Francis of Assisi, "The Canticle of the Sun," trans. by Bill Barrett from the Umbrian text of the Assisi codex at http://whitman.webster.edu/~barrettb/canticle.htm

2. Elizabeth O'Connor, *Eighth Day of Creation: Discovering Your Gifts and Using Them* (Washington, D.C.: Servant Leadership School, 1971), 19.

JOURNAL PAGE

JOURNAL PAGE

JOURNAL PAGE

JOURNAL PAGE

JOURNAL PAGE

JOURNAL PAGE

JOURNAL PAGE